LINEN AND LITURGY

The Story of the Marshall Family
and
The Parish Church
of
Keswick St. John

Margaret Armstrong
2002
PEEL WYKE PUBLICATIONS
22 Brandlehow Crescent
Keswick, CA12 4JE

Also by Margaret Armstrong
Thirlmere: Across the Bridges to Chapel
1849-1852
From the diary of Reverend Basil R. Lawson
Curate of Wythburn

1989

ISBN 0-9515173-1-7
Copyright M. Armstrong 2002
Printed by G. W. McKane & Son
KESWICK CUMBRIA
Published by PEEL WYKE PUBLICATIONS

CONTENTS

FOREWORD

The diary entry of Thomas Story Spedding for Thursday 27th December 1838 reads:

Cold, but fair: Consecration of the new church (to St. John). By the Deed read from the altar by the chancellor, Mary Ballentine Marshall was sole Foundress & Patroness.

The story of how that Church came to be founded and what has happened since is inextricably associated with the Marshall family. It is well worth telling. Now Margaret Armstrong, after painstaking research, has set out this story for us.

It used to be said that there was a Marshall on every lake. Now there is none left of this distinguished Lake District family. The personal history of the Marshalls is of substantial interest. But what is particularly worth recording is what they stood for in relation to the church which they had founded. In short, this was excellence in every sphere. It was their wish, which they implemented, that St. John's Church should have the best site in the area, the best architect, the best materials, organ and glass and, above all the best possible incumbents.

It is a great pleasure to record that at the present time St. John's is reaching a new high of excellence under the leadership of Canon Brian Smith, our present Vicar, and a dedicated team.

I commend this booklet to all who are interested in discovering how St. John's Church, with the powerful backing of the Marshall family, became such an important source of inspiration for proclaiming the Gospel to the people of Keswick, to our many visitors and to the wider world.

John Spedding

Mirehouse
Keswick
April 2002

PREFACE

IN FRIENDSHIP TOGETHER, WE RESOLVE TO WORSHIP GOD, SERVE THE COMMUNITY AND SHARE OUR FAITH IN JESUS CHRIST

This is the Mission Statement formulated by the Parochial Church Council of St. John's Church in November 1988 after a day of audit, prayer and discussion at Rydal Hall. Canon Brian Smith arranged that we should conduct a review of our church life so that we could set priorities and attainable targets. He invited Captain Jim Currin, of the Church Army, our Diocesan Officer for Evangelism to act as consultant and help in developing a strategy for the future to enable us to use our talents to the full in response to God's Spirit.

I would guess that the ideals put into the Mission Statement at the end of that day are the same as the desires of the Marshall family in founding and furthering the Church of Keswick St. John through four generations.

Brian, a former Royal Air Force Chaplain came to St. John's in 1995 after a long interregnum. The Parish had been well cared for by Canon Michael Braithwaite, then Rural Dean, Father Tony Hall, a retired priest, Parish Sister Irene of the Community of the Holy Name, and a devoted band of lay people, but everyone was looking for a fresh leader. Within a very short time the congregation knew that they had that man. He began by organising a thorough cleaning of the building. For three days, scores of people, swept, scrubbed, washed windows and polished woodwork. There was great enjoyment in working together. That fellowship has grown, still in caring for the building and churchyard but also in worship, study and leisure activities. All are encouraged to use their particular talents for God and our church family.

Knowing of my interest in local history, Brian asked me to bring up to date the leaflet, prepared by the late Canon Watson, for a guided tour of the church. From the research needed came a series of articles in the Parish Magazine. Supplemented with other material, a fascinating story has gradually evolved over four years. It is presented as a tribute to the Marshall family, the Patrons, the Clergy, the many Churchwardens (I had the honour of being the first lady to hold the office) and all those people who have so gladly served this church.

ACKNOWLEDGEMENTS

I thank John Spedding, Patron of the Parish Church of St. John the Evangelist, Keswick for writing the Foreword and for his interest and constructive help. I appreciate the continuous encouragement given by Canon Brian Smith. He made available to me all the books, papers and pictures stored in his Vicarage after the move from the old Parsonage. Some notes made by Canon Richard Watson were amongst the many documents. It seems that he was preparing a Parish History. The sources of his material were not indicated but he was a known historian and there is no reason to doubt the accuracy of the interesting sections that I have included. They are acknowledged in the text.

Thanks are due to archivists of the County Record Offices in Carlisle and Whitehaven and to librarians in Keswick and Leeds.

Louisa and Lewis Creed of York have supplied me with a great deal of material concerning the branch of the Marshall family descended from Susan Myers. I am grateful to them and have enjoyed their correspondence.

I thank Dr. D. W. Hadley for permission to use extracts from his notes on the stained glass windows of St. John's

Thanks to the University of Leeds Art Collection for permission to reproduce the John Russell Portraits of John and Jane Marshall: to the West Yorkshire Archive Service for producing for me a copy of the portrait of Henry Cowper Marshall and to the National Portrait Gallery for allowing me to copy the photograph, given to me by Louisa Creed, of Frederic William Henry Myers and his son, Leopold. Stephen Armstrong, Margaret Bowden and Stephnie Critchley have also supplied illustrations for which I thank them.

The advice and expertise of David Branthwaite, Keith Loan and Malcolm Rigg concerning printing and publication has been most valuable. G. W. McKane, David's great grandfather and founder of the firm was Churchwarden of St. John's in 1893 and their printing works have produced the Parish Magazines since 1923.

I would like to acknowledge the help that I have had from my family. My son, Phillip and my granddaughter Rachel have accompanied me on visits to Leeds and my second son, Stephen read and corrected the first draft. Irwin Bragg, my brother-in-law provided expert help with the illustrative material. Finally, I am deeply grateful to my husband, Harold for his endless patience during the many hours spent in libraries, in record offices and with my computer.

Margaret Armstrong

Keswick
April 2002

Chapter 1

Spinners and Builders

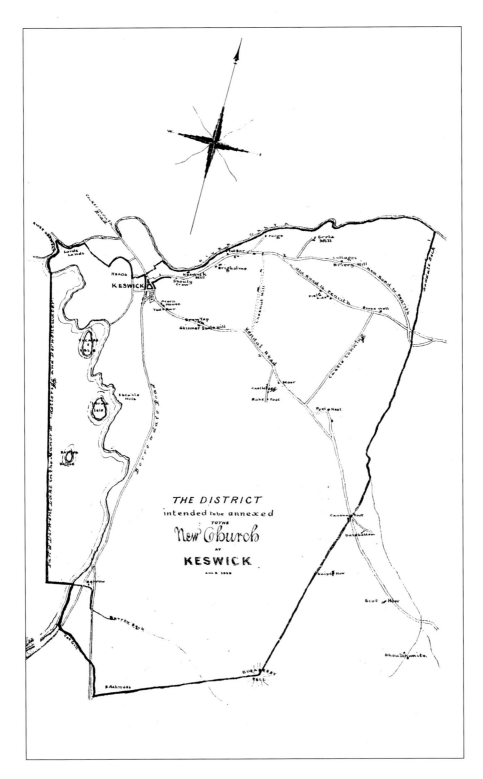

2

Before the main service on a Sunday morning, St. John's church is a busy place. The parishioners on duty are putting out hymn books and leaflets, ladies are arranging cups and saucers and preparing to serve refreshments, a corner is being set up with toys for the smallest children, the book stall is being organised, the music group may be there placing instruments and microphones. The server lights the altar candles, the choir leader takes a last rehearsal and there is a murmur of conversation as members of the congregation take their places.

Quietly, the acolytes and choir position themselves at the western end of the centre aisle. The leader holds the burnished cross, a potent symbol of the Christian faith and a reminder that the Celtic Saint Kentigern came in A.D. 553, to a thwaite or clearing, just to the north, planted a cross and preached the Gospel of Christ. Around the succession of churches later built there, was formed the ancient parish of Greater Crosthwaite, of which the present parish of Keswick St. John was a part. The clergy and choir are robed in a manner suggesting medieval clerical dress. Once, the land on which they stand belonged to the great Cistercian Fountains Abbey. The local place name 'grange' indicates that the monks had a farm of some kind nearby. Following the dissolution of the monasteries, the parish eventually became part of the estates of the Roman Catholic Radcliffe family, Earls of Derwentwater. When James Radcliffe, the third Earl was executed for supporting the Jacobite Rebellion in 1715, his estates passed to the Crown and were given to the Trustees of Greenwich Hospital for Seamen. In 1832 the Castlerigg estate was put up for sale and was bought by John Marshall, (1765-1845) a Leeds manufacturer.

The purchase began the sequence of events which, more than one hundred and sixty years later, determined that today the Anglican church dedicated to St. John the Evangelist is preparing to celebrate the Eucharist. The presiding priest comes to the lectern and welcomes the congregation. A sentence of scripture, a few moments of silent prayer and he joins the procession. Singing the opening hymn, they move down the centre aisle, passing over a slate stone with the incised initials J.M. Beneath this stone is the vault where the mortal remains of John Marshall's second son, also John, were laid to rest. He planned to build this new church for Keswick but died in 1836 when only the foundations were in position. His wife and family completed the construction.

The church with the churchyard, was consecrated by Hugh Percy, Lord Bishop of Carlisle on St. John's Day 1838. The square west tower was topped by eight graceful pinnacles, now lost, with the spire soaring from the midst of them and crowned with a weathervane cross. A six-sided vestry was exterior to the south east of the nave, which measured eighty feet in length and thirty feet wide. There was no sanctuary or side aisle. The windows were plain and the interior was simply furnished with the stone font and pulpit, which are still in use, as well as a communion table and a reading desk which have been replaced. It is possible that musicians used the balcony above the base of the tower as was the old custom, since there was no organ installed.

From this beginning the building has been the outward and visible sign of some constant and some changing ideas in worship and theology. There have been obvious additions and modifications but the real interest is to discover why St. John's came into being and how it has developed. To understand this it is necessary to study the religious and social climate of the times and to look at the people who, acting on their beliefs, desires and convictions of responsibility to God and humanity, produced the church, in its widest sense, which we are privileged to enjoy and serve today.

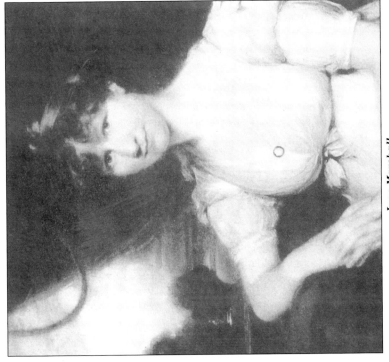

Jane Marshall
Portrait by John Russell, 1802

John Marshall
Portrait by John Russell, 1802

Reproduced by courtesy of the University of Leeds Arts Collection

4

In August 1795 John Marshall and his bride enjoyed a honeymoon in the Lake District. For part of that time they were in the Keswick area. The former Jane Pollard wrote to her great friend, Dorothy Wordsworth about the view of Bassenthwaite that she had seen from the top of a hill. In September Dorothy replied to Jane who was by then settling into her new home in Leeds, "I congratulate you upon your present felicity and happy prospects with heartfelt pleasure."

When the marriage took place John Marshall was already established as a flax-spinner with premises in Holbeck near Leeds. He came from a family of dissenters who refused to accept the doctrines of the established church and settled in the bleak valleys north of Leeds earning livings as clothiers, spinners and weavers. His father, Jeremiah moved into Leeds and became a successful linen draper. John born in 1765 was his only surviving child and after attending Hipperholme School in Halifax he learned accounting and French and entered his father's business at the age of seventeen. Jeremiah was a Baptist but joined Joseph Priestley's Unitarian, Mill Hill Chapel.

Priestley's reputation as a scientist influenced the young John Marshall. In 1787 Jeremiah died suddenly leaving no will. John found that profits from trade brought in more money than he needed. His interest had been aroused by experiments being carried out to discover if linen yarn could be spun by machinery. Using the surplus capital that he had, John leased premises near Adel, Leeds and began the firm that was to last almost a hundred years and generate great wealth for himself and his descendants.

Jane Marshall was one of the daughters of William Pollard, a mill owner and manufacturer of Halifax. He was a Unitarian, a staunch supporter of the Northgate-end Chapel there. Samuel Threlkeld, formerly Unitarian Minister at Penrith, was the pastor. His daughter, Elizabeth had been entrusted with the care of the motherless, Dorothy Wordsworth who spent nine years with the Threlkelds. Jane became Dorothy's constant companion and both were pupils at Hipperholme School. After Dorothy left Halifax, in 1787, the friends kept up a correspondence. In 1794 Dorothy, with William Wordsworth revisited Halifax. Jane was now the charming and beautiful fiancee of John Marshall. He and William became acquainted and began a friendship that continued for the rest of their lives. When, in the 1830's John was about to purchase a country estate for his son John Marshall II, he consulted William who suggested that he should buy the Castlerigg Manor lands and so determined the site on which our Church was built.

In 1828, John Marshall II married Mary Ballantine Dykes of Dovenby Hall. The union with a family of Cumberland gentry was a source of great satisfaction for his father.

John Marshall, now aged sixty-three, had prospered. During the wars with France, through skilled management and having had the foresight to stock his warehouses with flax, he was able to manufacture linen thread when others could not. By the end of the war in 1815 he had made his fortune. He invested shrewdly at home and abroad. His profit bought land and houses, mostly in the Lake District. He acquired the Patterdale estates of Mounsey, the so-called "Last King of Patterdale" and built Hallsteads at Watermillock on the shores of Ullswater. Here he entertained during the summer months and many connections were made with prominent people from near and far. Sir Walter Scott and George Canning came with William Wordsworth to "Mr. Marshall's elegant villa near Lyulph's tower".

He was appointed High Sheriff of Cumberland in 1821. The next step was to obtain a seat in parliament. This was accomplished by buying his way in as was the custom before the reform act of 1832. Being a Whig, a dissenter, a bluff northerner and not a good speaker, John Marshall was ill at ease in London. He was an M.P. for only four years, resigning his seat in 1830. Nevertheless he bought a house in Grosvenor Square and the family were able to enjoy the London Season.

Between 1796 and 1814 twelve children were born to John and Jane Marshall. The first son, William became a lawyer but John, the second son entered the family business at the age of seventeen. Five years later, in 1820, he was made a partner. After John's marriage his father built a home for him at Headingly, Leeds and then financed the purchase of the Castlerigg estates in 1832.

In the same year John II was a candidate in the first election for Leeds. He was a natural Liberal choice, a Unitarian, a reformer, a townsman and a great employer of labour who could represent the town's economic interest and he was duly elected.

William Wordsworth had suggested that John II might build a house near Broomhill Point and in 1833 the architect Anthony Salvin (1799-1881) prepared drawings for a country house but it did not reach the planning stage.

From Canon Richard Watson's notes :-

"Keswick and its neighbourhood formed part of the extensive parish of Crosthwaite; but it was already clear that some other arrangement would be necessary. For one thing, a new town was beginning to grow, and the expansion was moving the centre of population inconveniently far from Crosthwaite. In 1835 an indication had been given of the need for a new parish church when the Rev. J. Bush, curate of Crosthwaite and later Vicar of Buttermere, began to hold services on Sunday evenings in the Town Hall. The congregations were too large for the hall. At the same time the official provision made for the spiritual care of Keswick was hardly adequate, even by the standard of those days. The Vicar of Crosthwaite, who was also Rector of Caldbeck, was not resident in either parish; having obtained five years leave of absence, he had removed to Gateshead, leaving his parishes in the care of curates."

"A series of letters, dated May 1835 - April 1836, from Mr. Marshall to Mr. Joshua Stanger of Keswick, and also to the Bishop of Carlisle, show that first he hoped to share the task with Mr. Stanger and others. But serious differences arose which could not be resolved, and in the end Mr. Marshall abandoned his plans for a house and undertook sole responsibility for the church."

John Marshall asked Salvin to prepare plans for a church in the Early English style. The watercolour print prepared in his office showing how the new church would look is in the County Record Office in Carlisle.

A Church Building Act in 1818 had set in motion the building of new churches with the provision of one million pounds. Six years later a further half million was granted and by 1840 more than 600 "Commissioners Churches" as they came to be called were built. Many others were erected with private finance. The motivation for this was not entirely altruistic. Many of the well-to-do regarded the Church as a means of controlling the possibly revolutionary poor. Some, including the Marshalls believed sincerely in spiritual and practical education, at least, for the hardworking and deserving members of the growing populace. John Marshall was part of a Whig Parliament that co-operated with the Conservative leader, Peel to bring forward measures necessary for church reform. The ideas debated are also likely to have influenced him in the decision to build St. John's but fate intervened. After a short illness, he died in London in 1836.

The foundations of the new church in Keswick were already in place and there seems to have been no doubt that the construction should continue. Records in the Book of the Trustees for Saint John's Church indicate the legal position. In 1838 when Reginald Dykes Marshall the son of John II was six years old, his mother Mary Ballantine Marshall and his uncles, Henry Cowper Marshall and Lamplugh Brougham Dykes of Dovenby Hall were his guardians. Also acting for him and administering the estate that he had inherited were his father's other brothers William of Patterdale Hall and James Garth of Monk Coniston.

From the Book of Trustees:- "Conveyed to Her Majesty's Commissioners for building new churches and their successors, land, when consecrated, to be devoted to Ecclesiastical purposes for ever." One hundred and ten pounds was paid to Frechville Lawson Ballantine Dykes, James Garth Marshall and Henry Cowper Marshall as Trustees for the land.

The records continue with the reasons for building:- "The population of Crosthwaite Parish at the last return was 4344. All places of public worship in the parish will only hold 1785 persons. Mary Ballantine Marshall for the spiritual advantages of inhabitants who reside at an inconvenient distance from the parish church and other places of worship hath at her own cost erected and built a chapel for the Honour of Almighty God and for the celebration of divine worship according to the rites of the United Church of England and Ireland."

It was contemplated that a district would be assigned to the new chapel which was generously endowed for an incumbent and repairs. The seating capacity was estimated as 405 places of which 116 must be free. Her Majesty's Commissioners were satisfied and Hugh Percy, Bishop of Carlisle consecrated the church and graveyard.

From Canon Richard Watson's notes.

"In September 1836 prices for the new Church now building in Keswick were:-

Thomas Roper of Lamonby	:	*Free stone 4d per cubic foot, the stone to be in rough blocks not exceeding 12 feet.*
Joseph Barren and others	:	*Leading free stone from Lamonby to site of new Church 9/2d per ton.*
John Hewitson of Keswick	:	*Quarrying the stone at Castle Head for the rough walling at 9d per cubic yard.*
William Clark and others	:	*Leading stones from Castle Head to site at 9d per cubic yard.* *Loading and leading sand from the field adjoining Castle Head to site 9d per cubic yard.*
Thomas Briggs	:	*Digging out foundations and levelling at 4d per cubic yard.*
Jos. Watson of Brigham	:	*Lime 8/6d per load of 7 bushels at the new Church.*

The Clerk of Works was a Mr. Bonner.

Anthony Salvin who had worked on Windsor Castle, the Tower of London, Caernarvan, Newark, Warwick and Alnwick Castles as well as building new churches and the County Hotel in Carlisle, stated on the 18th October that slate from Eskdale would cost 52/- per ton; delivered from Whitehaven then carriage to Keswick would be about 10/- per ton more . . . "I like the colour well . . ."

The total cost of the building was £4103.

By August 1838 the pews were being let to residents of the district and Robert Southey, the poet Laureate, a regular worshipper was elected Chairman of the pewholders."

Soon afterwards the remains of the late John Marshall were removed from London and interred in the family vault. Mary Ballantine Marshall conveyed to her son Reginald Dykes Marshall, through his trustees, the right to nominate a minister. The Reverend Frederic Myers was nominated and became the first incumbent of the Church of Saint John the Evangelist in Keswick.

Hallsteads, Ullswater. Home of John Marshall I
Extended and used as an outward bound centre

The Parsonage

Chapter 2

A Radical Divine and a Guardian Mayor

The Reverend Frederic Myers, was one of a new breed of clergyman prepared for an altering situation in the Anglican church. Born in 1811 he was educated by his father who was on the staff of the Military Academy, Woolwich. At Clare Hall, Cambridge, Frederic became a Fellow and gained many honours including a Hebrew Scholarship.

In the preface to his book "Catholic Thoughts on the Bible and Theology", first printed in 1834, he wrote "the primary idea of the Church of Christ is that of a Brotherhood of men worshipping Christ as their revelation of the Highest; and that equality of spiritual privileges is so characteristic of its constitution that the existence of any priestly caste in it is destructive of it; and also that the faith which it should make obligatory on its members is emphatically faith in Christ Himself . . . and very subordinately only in any definite theoretic creed."

Myers was ordained in 1835 and to quote his own words, fully aware of the "excitement of ecclesiastical fever" at the time. The established Church of England was being challenged, particularly in the new industrial areas, by Baptists, Unitarians, Methodists and immigrant Irish Catholics. Politically, many middle class radicals and Whigs objected to the Anglican Church's control of public life especially when the Bishops blocked parliamentary reform. Followers of the 'Oxford Movement' were also anti-establishment. However, many clergy including Myers were aware that change must come from within.

After almost three years as a curate in Lincolnshire, Frederic Myers was offered the incumbency of the Parish Church at Leeds. He declined and instead took the opportunity to come to Keswick where, with the approval of his patrons, he could put into practice his own ideas of theology and spiritual oversight. He maintained that the Bible was only part of God's revelation to man. It was a record of that revelation through the Jewish vision of God as Monarch, Lawgiver and Judge, to the Christian view of God the Father, Redeemer and Sanctifier, coming to the fullest image of God in Jesus Christ. He saw around him much that was unjust in society and hoped that Christianity could be an agent for change. He believed in individual responsibility and the equal potential of all souls. He looked to the future but nevertheless held that modern interpretations of spirituality should not interfere with basic Christian tenets.

In 1838, the new district church of Saint John could be seen clearly for miles around Keswick. The building of fresh pink sandstone from quarries in the Eden valley was in the midst of green fields with few dwellings or trees to obstruct the sight of it, from Derwentwater or the surrounding fells.

Frederic Myers, preached his first sermon on September 9th. To quote his own opening words, "We meet for the first time today to offer up worship to God in a new temple; a temple as it appears to me, erected in exact accordance with the spirit of our Church's Prayers, neither rejecting all aid of art, nor encouraging sensuous worship, impressively simple and beautiful exceedingly."

He concludes this section,"Before all things would I have us to remember that this house has been erected to God's honour not our own, that herein without a rival Christ Jesus is to be exalted as the Lord, and that though christian instruction may justly be blended with other christian acts, the primary object of a temple must ever be a place of worship, a house of prayer and not of preaching."

Immediately, he began to devote himself to the needs of his parishioners. As well as good Christians he aimed to make them good citizens.

Thomas Story Spedding, a trustee of St. John's and a kinsman of our present Patron wrote in his diary for March 3rd 1840 about a conversation he had with the new incumbent. "Myers spoke much about his own pastoral proceedings. Many of them vehemently contra. He in truth no conservative Divine, rather a

Frederic Myers' Memorial Window given by his widow Susan Marshall 1889
designed by
Henry Holiday and made by Powell & Son
Holiday re-used this design about 30 years later at Symondsbury, Dorset

little confident and egotistical, yet fundamentally wise and good. Probably a good deal of youthful zeal and hope will yield to experience. A most agreeable man to exchange ideas, with candid and tolerant, ex animo, and far above cant in any of its forms."

A room was built near the church (eventually to become part of St. John's school) where the parishioners would have provided, as Myers said, the two things most needful for man, the means of personal improvement and the means of social intercourse."

There was to be a school on Sundays for children over seven and on weekdays for children from two to seven years of age. On Saturday mornings Mr. Myers ran a Provident Club and on Wednesday evenings he organised lectures of literary, social or scientific interest. He made available books, maps and specimens for the study of natural history. These activities were the seeds from whence grew the Keswick Library, the Museum, the Lecture and other Societies existing today.

Frederic Myers came to Keswick a bachelor but evidently the Marshall family anticipated that he would marry and the church architect Anthony Salvin was asked to design a parsonage. He prepared a plan. The specification for building is now in the County Record Office at Whitehaven and yields some interesting details.

The foundations and walling stone were to come from the local quarry at Castlehead. String course labels and copings to be Coniston flag stones. These also to be used for the kitchen floor but Borrowdale flags could be used for the cellar floor. Window frames to be of fir wood with oak sills. Chimney flues to be built with great care and chimney pieces in the Study, Dining and Drawing rooms to be plain marble at a cost of £6 each. W.C.'s to have mahogany seats and flaps. The general instruction was for all materials and labour to be of the best. Cost was estimated at £840.00. It must have been underestimated. From the parish Magazine of May 1889, "The Dowager Lady Mounteagle who died in April was one of the munificent benefactors who so generously contributed to the Parish of St. John's from its beginning. She built the parsonage in 1838 at a cost of £1630; and recently increased the endowment by a gift of £1800. She always had a keen interest in the parish and its welfare."

In October 1839, Frederic Myers brought his bride, Fanny Calcroft to her new home but his happiness was shortlived. Fanny died in January 1840. Her name is the first on the Myers' family tomb, which is on the right hand side of the gateway to the churchyard coming from the new vicarage.

In 1842, two years after his young wife Fanny died childless, Frederic Myers married Susan Harriet Marshall, youngest sister of the founder of St. John's. Her mother, Jane, already deeply involved in the church which held memories of her second son, John, now had an added interest in its progress. Furthermore her fourth son, Henry Cowper Marshall, in 1844 bought Derwent Island and began to improve the house that was there.

From the early 1840s Jane and John Marshall left the running of the mills in Leeds to their sons and spent most of their declining years at Hallsteads beside Ullswater. John Marshall died in 1845. When Jane died in 1847 her bequests showed her concern for the parish work of her son-in-law Frederic and his wife, Susan. She left money for St. John's Church and for an infants' school. £500 was left to Frederic Myers, to be used as he thought fit. He invested the money for increasing the stipends of poor clergymen, increasing the salaries of masters and mistresses of schools for the education of the poorer classes, supporting schools by the donation of books and apparatus, distributing awards to pupils and establishing village libraries and mutual improvement societies.

14

Frederic W. H. Myers (1843-1901) and his son Leopold Myers (1881-1944)
by courtesy of The National Portrait Gallery, London
Photograph by Eveleen Myers

On 20th September 1848 Frederic Myers purchased the land near to St. John's Church for a public library for Keswick. He saw it built and operating but it was left to his curate, T. D. Harford Battersby, when he became incumbent in 1851 after Myers death, to develop the library and later add the lecture hall on land bought by Susan Myers.

With her three sons, Susan moved away. The eldest Frederic William Henry Myers became a minor poet and was a founder member of the Society for Psychical Research. In later life he wrote how as a child he thought that beyond St. John's Parsonage garden he would enter paradise. All of the Myers family have memorials in the chancel, perhaps the most beautiful is the window showing The Good Shepherd, The Sower and The Lost Piece of Silver given by Susan Myers in 1889. She died in 1896 aged 85, some 45 years after she left the Parsonage. From St. John's Magazine for that date, "she is still affectionately remembered by those who then lived and are living now, for her kindness in the parish and for the generous way in which she aided her husband in carrying out his wise and philanthropic schemes for the good of the people of Keswick."

Anyone who sits in the choir stalls, or polishes the warm mature oak and the brasses in the chancel of St. John's Church, will have read on the front row of the north side, "IN MEMORY OF HENRY COWPER MARSHALL TO WHOSE CARE AND FORETHOUGHT WORSHIPPERS OF THIS CHURCH ARE MUCH INDEBTED".

Henry Cowper Marshall died in 1884, five years before the extension of the chancel was completed. His death ended an association with St. John's which began when he became one of the guardians of his older brother John's son, Reginald Dykes Marshall. He helped to administer the estates that the seven year old inherited and acted for him after the widowed Mary Ballantyne Marshall transferred the patronage of the new church to her son.

Henry, born in 1808, was the fourth son of John and Jane Marshall. He grew up in Leeds and in 1828 joined his brothers John and James, in the family firm of Marshall & Co. Flax-Spinners. While the older brothers were interested in the machinery and processing of flax, Henry was much more concerned with the commercial development of the firm and when John died, took over almost all the buying and selling, keeping meticulous records as his father had done. The success of the firm made the family very wealthy.

At the age of twenty-nine Henry married Catherine Lucy Spring-Rice, youngest daughter of the Chancellor of the Exchequer. The marriage was obviously a social and political triumph. Within a short time Henry became an Alderman and then in 1843, Mayor of Leeds. With a growing family, he was looking for a country estate when Derwent Island with a remarkable house built by Joseph Pocklington, a member of a wealthy Nottinghamshire banking family, came on the market. Henry bought it. He immediately employed Anthony Salvin, who had remodelled Patterdale Hall for his oldest brother, William, and designed St. John's Church and Parsonage, to alter the house. Fresh water was piped in under the lake and a fleet of boats ferried people, provisions and coal to and fro. Up to twenty servants, sometimes brought from Leeds, dwelt in the cellars and served the family.

Seven of the children of John and Jane Marshall had married and produced offspring. By the late 1840's they had thirty-eight grandchildren. The family was close and Henry's children had many cousins sharing their summers. The now silent island must once have been alive with children shouting and playing together. Henry, with his statistical mind measured the height of the growing flock each year.

Some of John and Jane Marshall's grandchildren must surely have been rowed across to St. John's Church to the service, and afterwards visited their Aunt Susan Myers in the Parsonage. There may have been more than one, who, like their cousin Frederic Myers, thought that in the hills beyond the garden was Paradise.

The National Census of March 1851 lists the inhabitants of St. John's Parsonage as:- Frederic Myers 39, Perpetual Curate, Susan Myers 39, wife, then two sons, Frederic W. H. 8 and Ernest J. and also four female servants. Unfortunately Frederic Myers was already a sick man and his curate, Thomas Dundas Harford Battersby had been in charge of St. John's for several months in 1850. When Frederic Myers died in July 1851 after thirteen years of devoted ministry, Battersby was the natural choice as the next incumbent.

Born in 1822, Thomas was the third son of J. S. Harford Battersby and his wife, Elizabeth Grey Dundas. In 1841 he was at Oxford and expected to follow his father into banking. In his first year he was a wavering man but in the next year made Christian friends and with some of them spent the long vacation of 1843 at Grasmere reading and climbing. During this summer he met Coleridge, and Wordsworth, who was then Poet Laureate, and living at Rydal. The young student admired both but later felt that Coleridge had led him astray.

Battersby was deeply impressed by the earnestness, sincerity and holiness of the leaders of the Oxford Movement, Newman, Manning, Pusey and Keble whose ideas were strongly Anglo-Catholic. It was after listening to a sermon by Archdeacon Manning that he decided to take Holy Orders. After some years travelling abroad he was ordained and became Curate at Gosport in 1847. His mind was troubled and he was undecided whether to follow Evangelical or Tractarian teaching, when he read Frederick Myers books on theology. Battersby heard that Myers was looking for a curate, came to Keswick to visit and arranged to join him, having been persuaded of the truth of Protestant rather than Anglo-Catholic principles.

According to the memoirs written years later by Battersby's sons he found the new church already well organised and provided with all the means and apparatus of improvement and having a congregation of sober, thoughtful people". He said that Myers was a model of forbearance, kindness and friendliness but that his teaching, in a desire to be catholic was inclined to be indefinite. The poor in the parish, Battersby noted, had gone to the Plymouth Brethren "who are strong and have an admirable minister."

Henry Marshall offered Battersby the living, which he accepted and was to hold for thirty three momentous years. Benjamin Hodgson, who was the Sexton for twenty-seven years from 1838 has at least one family member in the present congregation. All the faithful must have been gratified when St. John's was separated from Crosthwaite and the district assigned became an independent parish in 1856.

Just about this time there was another generous Marshall legacy. In 1848 Cordelia, the third daughter of John and Jane Marshall made her will, leaving £1000 to St. John's Church and £2000 to the endowment of St. John's School. The interest from this money was first to be applied to necessary repairs and second to the payment of salary for a schoolmistress. Cordelia had married in 1841, William Whewell, Professor of Moral Philosophy at Cambridge. In the same year he was appointed Master of Trinity College in succession to Christopher Wordsworth. Cordelia died in 1853 but the will that she left did not take effect until 1866 on the death of Dr. Whewell when his life interest in the property terminated.

Everything was set for expansion of the building and ministry.

Henry Cowper Marshall (1808-1884) Mayor of Leeds 1843
© Reproduced by kind permission of West Yorkshire Archive Service

Chapter 3

Evangelism
and
Expansion

Ten years after accepting the living at St. John's, the Census returns of 1861 show Thomas Dundas Harford Battersby, Perpetual Curate, as the head of a busy household in the Parsonage. He was thirty-eight years old as was his wife Mary Forbes, from Edinburgh. They were married in 1854 and there were now three sons, John, Dundas and George aged three, two and one. On the day of the Census, Mary's two younger sisters, Elizabeth, twenty years old and Dorothy, eighteen were visiting from Scotland. Also in the house were the staff, a cook, a housemaid, a general servant, a nurse and a nursery maid.

In December the same year a daughter was born and given the names of her mother and grandmother, Mary, Elizabeth. A fourth son, Alfred made the family complete in 1865.

Thomas Battersby sought first and foremost to fulfil the high aims of his predecessor. In 1855 a lecture hall was added to the library. Here he began a "Mechanics Institute", then Keswick Literary and Scientific Society and eventually all kinds of classes. Concerned for the public health, with a Dr. Leitch and John Fisher Crosthwaite he formed a small waterworks company and opened up a supply of water from Skiddaw, for the townspeople.

His teaching was always evangelical based on sound reasoning and a study of the scriptures. He condemned the 'Broadchurch' view that reason and conscience only should dictate what doctrine was accepted saying "only spiritual men can judge spiritual things." In his view, the High church and ritualistic movement should be met by the energy and spirituality of the Evangelicals. Battersby became convinced that only by uniting with others in parish, diocese and church could work be done that was widespread and lasting. He went to meetings of the Evangelical Alliance and attended conferences in Amsterdam and Basle. He was with Robert Wilson, a member of the Society of Friends, from Broughton Grange, near Cockermouth, when, at a Convention in Oxford, he believed that he had a revelation of Christ. Afterwards, Battersby wrote "He was all that I wanted". He felt humbled and at peace.

With Robert Wilson, Battersby decided to promote a religious convention in Keswick. He sent out invitations to three days of "Union Meetings for the Promotion of Practical Holiness" to Christians of every section of the Church of God. The first meeting in the grounds of the Parsonage was undermined after a prominent American speaker, Pearsall Smith, withdrew at the last minute. However, it went ahead and was followed by another in the next month, July 1875 when a hired tent was erected in Eskin Street. There were storms and the tent collapsed. For the first but not the last time the meetings had to be held in halls around the town. Nothing could stop the movement, which has flourished and grown ever since.

Enlivened by the personality of Battersby and by the love and respect the Keswick townspeople had for Mary, his wife, the congregation at St. John's steadily increased. Other factors, such as the church schools, the population growth in the town, the coming of the railway and the general climate of Victorian religious observance must also have influenced the decisions to enlarge the original building. The north aisle was constructed in 1862, the south aisle added in 1882 and consecrated by Bishop Harvey Goodwin of Carlisle. He recalled that as a young man he taught in St. John's Sunday School.

All was planned for the Convention of July 1883 but even as people were arriving at the station, the sad news that the founder had died at his home was passed from one to another.

A few days later over one thousand people assembled in the Convention tent and marched to St. John's Churchyard. One hundred robed clergy were present at the funeral with Canon Battersby's family and parishioners. His body was laid to rest outside the west end of the new south aisle. His passing marked the end of a remarkable era at St. Johns.

The death of Canon Battersby was an occasion of great sadness but also a time to give thanks for his devotion to his parish of Keswick St. John and to the wider sphere of the Evangelical Alliance and the founding of the Keswick Convention. The newly appointed Vicar of Crosthwaite, Reverend H. D. Rawnsley wrote in his Parish Magazine for August that he felt "deep regret that the Pastor of St. John's Church has been in the last month called to his rest. No neighbourhood can spare an example of consistent piety and conscientious labour for God and brethren: when that exemplar has been a presence among men for thirty-two years, the loss is a grievous one indeed. Much has been said that we all wished to hear the unselfish life that has served Keswick for so long. Too little perhaps of the debt, in the department of public works, that Keswick owes to the memory of the late Canon Battersby. No one willingly incurs lengthened opposition from his fellow men, even if he foresees that what he is striving for is for the public advantage. Good sanitation and pure water are especially the advantages that any place of public resort for visitors must aim at. "And whilst those who enjoy those advantages now at Keswick may be proud of them. We are as little likely to forget the brave men who fought for them - and foremost of these was the revered Vicar of St. John's."

Later that year St. John's had a new vicar, the Reverend J. N. Hoare, M. A., and church life moved on. The Parish Magazine for December 1884, which cost ONE PENNY, shows the services as, Holy Communion, on each Sunday at varying times. On Christmas Day there were two Communion services and on the last day of the year a Service and Sermon at 8 p.m. There must have been a room available for worship at The Forge, for each Sunday at 6.30 services were held. During the week there were Cottage Lectures, Mothers' Meetings', Band of Hope, Sunday School Teachers' Class, Childrens' Work Party and Clothing Clubs as well as a regular Choir Practice. There was an active Temperance Society and a Young Womens' Association. The church was a great centre of community life.

The same magazine gives a report on the Sunday Schools which were held at St. John's and at Brigham School. Mr. Postlethwaite was Superintendent of St. John's and Mr. Highton Superintendent of Brigham. The teachers undertook to find a substitute if they were unable to attend on any Sunday and also to visit the homes of children who were absent more than once. Children were required to attend a place of worship as well, on Sunday, unless they brought a letter from their parents exempting them.

Each Sunday a child might receive a maximum of six marks, one for punctual attendance, one for learning the lesson, two for good conduct and two for attendance at morning service. It would seem a rigorous regime. Questions were set each month, which would appear to tax many an adult. For instance:- "Show that the "Ordering" of priests took place in Apostolic times" and "What temptations befell David in the Kingdom of Acish?"

Collections were made for prizes, which were awarded to the best scholars and also probably to those gaining top marks. Recently a St. John's Sunday School prize came to light in a Charity shop in Keswick. It was awarded to Ethel Dalzell at Christmas 1890 and signed, John N. Hoare, Vicar. A small brown hard backed volume with a coloured cover showing butterflies and flowers, it was bought from the Religious Tract Society and contains a moral tale entitled "The Mysterious House" by Mrs. Walton.

At the end of 1884, £150 from the Harford-Battersby Memorial fund was offered to the Trustee of the Library, to be expended upon the improvement and enlargement of the Lecture Hall. "- subject to the condition that it be called the Battersby Lecture Hall and that a tablet be placed in it to the memory of the founder."

Even when Canon Battersby had opened the new South Aisle in 1882 he was already thinking of more that needed to be done. He mentioned that if they had some more liberal gifts, the extension of the Chancel would be a great improvement architecturally to the Church since the addition of the new aisles.

Very much concerned with the projects and possibilities for the church was a representative of the third generation of the Marshall family. When his father died in 1836 without ever seeing more than the foundations of the church he planned, Reginald Dykes Marshall was only four years old. Throughout his minority his uncles, in particular Henry Cowper Marshall of Derwent Island carried out his duties as Trustee and Patron of St. John's for him.

Reginald Dykes Marshall joined the family business of flax spinners in Leeds when he was twenty-two after leaving Trinity College. The enterprise begun by his grandfather had already passed its peak of success. The second generation had been brought up to be country gentlemen and although they made considerable contributions to civic duties and reforms, were more interested in taking money out of the firm than in expanding it. There is little evidence that Reginald, the first of the Marshall grandchildren to enter the firm, ever saw his future in commerce. He knew that eventually he would inherit his father's estates and at the age of thirty-eight took his money out of the failing business and retired to Keswick to manage his land and property.

His impact on St. John's Church was immediate and obvious. He determined that a fitting memorial to his father would be a window of stained glass at the east end. Reginald may have become acquainted with Henry Holiday, the principal designer of stained glass for the old established London firm, Powell and Son, since Holiday was a frequent visitor to the Lake District. He appears to have been a sociable man and his friendships resulted in many commissions for windows.

In May 1879 Henry Holiday placed an order with Powell and Son for the East window of St. John's Church, Keswick, the bill to be sent to R. Marshall, Esq., The Cottage, Keswick. The specification was for six lancets; the centre lights to be Crucifixion and Resurrection, Isaac and Jonah below and Archangels above; the side-lights to have Angels at the top, Christ and Nicodemus, Christ and the Woman of Samaria, Christ opening the eyes of the blind and his charge to Saint Peter. At the base of the side-lights to be Naaman, Ruth, Isaiah and David. Also in the window, to be twelve texts.

The estimate for making was £238.16.0d. Holiday would charge almost as much again for providing the design, with the texts by another designer costing £3.3.8d.

Although the East window as a whole is a new design, Holiday had used some of the figures earlier. Isaac started life at Trinity College, Cambridge c.1871 as Onesimus and Jonah was originally Jeremiah at Grantchester. Unfortunately at the time that the east window was produced Powells were experimenting with new fluxes to assist the applied pigment to fire with the background glass. Most of the experiments were unsuccessful and some of the pigment has, over the years become detached. This is the reason for the scaly appearance of some parts of the window today.

In September 1879 the new window, a memorial to John Marshall, founder of the church was fixed in place.

In January 1887, the Vicar, Reverend J. N. Hoare and his Churchwardens announced that at the next Vestry Meeting they would lay before the parishioners of St. John's a sketch of the proposed alterations at the cast end of the church.

He had communicated with the Patron, Reginald Dykes Marshall who replied:-

"MY DEAR HOARE

I have been much pleased to hear that there exists in the parish a strong feeling that some change should be made in the arrangement of the East End of the Church. The plan of seats there has never been agreeable to my personal feelings, nor in accordance with my ideas of what is fitting; and, as patron of the living, I shall be glad to help (to a small extent) the congregation in remodelling that part of the Church and putting it into a condition more in accordance with the religious feeling of the time.

I trust you will have no difficulty in finding means for carrying out the work in a substantial and suitable manner; and I may add that Mrs. Marshall will do her best to further this object by organising a bazaar for the purpose some time next year.

Believe me.

Yours sincerely,

REGINALD DYKES MARSHALL."

By March of the same year fund raising was progressing with a list of all donations published in the magazine. These ranged from £100, down to 3 pence. The Bishop of Carlisle and the Bishop of Liverpool sent money and many parishioners had their gifts publicly acknowledged, something that would probably not be considered appropriate today.

The Bazaar was planned for August with the Lady Jane Spedding, Mrs. R. D. Marshall and her daughters, Rosamund and Sybil as well as Mrs. Hoare presiding at stalls. Arrangements were set out in the July magazine as well as a list of eighty people who had taken collecting cards for the general fund. All was a great success and £477.11s.3d., was raised, a considerable sum if translated into current values.

The Faculty for extending the chancel and building an organ chamber was granted in October 1888. By May 1889 the Vicar and Churchwardens were able to announce that a total of £1,413.1s.4d. was available, including £50 from the Diocesan Church Extension fund and £100 from the sale of the original organ. The chancel opened free from debt.

The Bishop of Carlisle, Harvey Goodwin came in July to open the extension. In his address he said "It is some fifty years since I first came to Keswick. I had just taken my degree, and I came here with a reading party. I think that the three months I then spent, were among the happiest in my long life. This was the church in which I always worshipped." He went on to speak of the gradual growth of the church. He remembered it as originally built, had seen it enlarged by the addition of the two aisles to meet the growing requirements of the parish and had now come to dedicate the chancel and consecrate extra ground for burials. When he first came to St. John's, he recalled, there were only two graves in the churchyard. One of them was that of the young wife of the incumbent, Frederic Myers and the other was the little daughter of the house on Derwent Island.

The space gained by the addition to the chancel was of service on the Sunday following its dedication, when there were 783 communicants, who were able to pass freely to and fro, while four clergymen served at the Lord's table.

T. D. H. Battersby
Vicar 1851 - 1883

M. L. C. Headlam, M.A.
Vicar 1906 - 1918

C. H. Lewin, M.A.
Vicar 1918 - 1935

V. M. Spencer-Ellis
Vicar 1950 - 1983

ST. JOHN'S PIERROTS - c.1930

Back row l-r: Jenny Davidson, Andy Edmondson, Edwin Kelly, Martha Stanley

Seated: Alan Tremble, Doris Kelly, Mirehouse Davidson, Elsie Burnyeat, Jack Bowden, Margaret Nicol (Bowden), George Read

Reproduced by courtesy of Mrs. Margaret Bowden

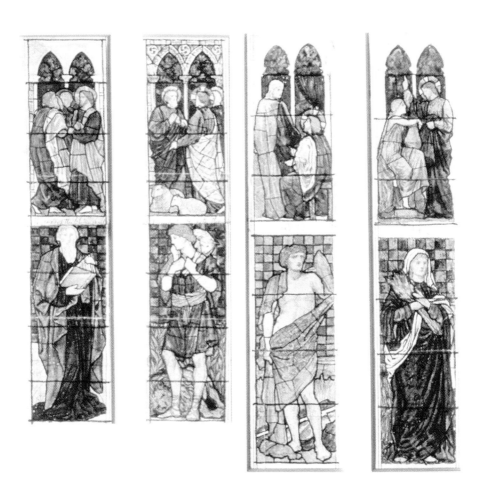

Above L-R Christ Opening the Eyes of the Blind
Christ's Charge to Peter 'Feed my Lambs'
Christ and Nicodemus
Christ and the Woman of Samaria

Below L-R Isaiah
David
Naaman
Ruth

From sketch design of east window by Henry Holiday. Details of faces not shown. Two alternative styles offered for the heads of lights: angels or geometrical pattern. Background left unfinished in some scenes. Client would understand that it would be similar to finished designs. East window as a whole was a new design but some figures had been used earlier. Isaac started life at Trinity College, Cambridge c.1871 as Onesimus, Jonah was originally Jeremiah at Grantchester

Crucifixion and resurrection

Isaac and Jonah

27

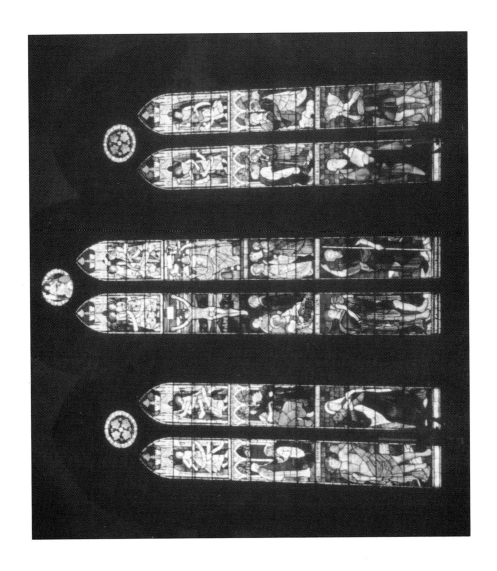

The East Window
Memorial
John Marshall II
founder of
St. John's Church,
designer
Henry Holiday,
made by
Powell & Son

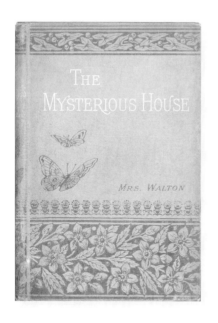

Ethel Dalzell
Sunday School Prize
S John's. Keswick.
Christmas 1890.

"Let Gran sing!" he pleaded.

THE
MYSTERIOUS HOUSE.

BY
MRS. WALTON,
AUTHOR OF
"A PEEP BEHIND THE SCENES," "LITTLE DOT,"
"CHRISTIE'S OLD ORGAN," &c.

London:
THE RELIGIOUS TRACT SOCIETY,
56, PATERNOSTER ROW; 65, ST. PAUL'S CHURCHYARD
AND 164, PICCADILLY

Chapter 4

Rituals and Candles, Colour and Music

These sanctuary windows placed in memory of Jane, the founder's mother and her sisters Ann and Ellen Pollard, her daughters Marianne, Lady Monteagle, Cordelia Whewell and Ellen Marshall who helped to carry forward the good work begun in the foundation of the church

Holiday Designs by Powell & Son from Stock

John and Matthew designed for Chipping Barnet in 1882

Mark and Luke from Trinity College, Cambridge. Luke was originally Nathaniel and Mark was Dante

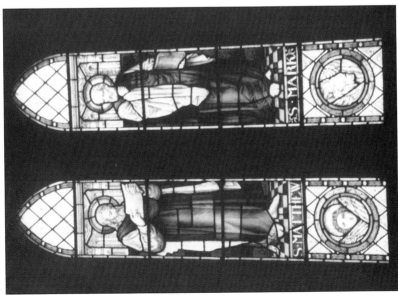

In 1890 one of the daughters of Reginald Dykes Marshall, Margaret Alice Marshall was married to Henry Arthur Whately by the Lord Bishop of Carlisle assisted by the Vicar of St. John's. A paragraph in the parish magazine for May notes that the church was beautifully decorated with flowers and the service was choral. "It is the first marriage in St. John's church of a grand-daughter of the founder, and we are glad to think that the chancel was ready, and part of the organ playable for the occasion." The oak choir stalls ordered by the architect of the extension, William Marshall, and dedicated to the memory of his father, Henry Cowper Marshall were in position and also the black and white marble floor. A brass tablet near the pulpit indicates that the floor became a memorial to Margaret Mitchell who died on Christmas Day 1889. Beside the east door there is another memorial which shows that this lady was a member of the mothers' meeting group and evidently a worker for the church. In the Crosthwaite Parish Magazine Canon Rawnsley marked her passing with a verse in which he says that she was "Dorcas-minded".

Reginald Marshall retired from the family firm, Marshalls of Leeds in 1872. He acquired Castlerigg Manor House and came to live there. The Fentons of Leeds built the house about 1840 and their coat of arms can be seen under the first floor window of the tower. Members of the Fenton family were business associates of the Marshalls. They sold the house to the Ledger family who constructed the magnificent stone terrace overlooking the gardens. It is said that they became bankrupt in doing so. Reginald Dykes Marshall took the opportunity to buy the property, possibly so that as Lord of the Manor of Castlerigg he might dwell in the manor house which his father never did since he chose to build St. John's Church instead of a home for his family. The Census returns for 1891 show him living there in some style. He was fifty-eight years old and a J.P. Also at Castlerigg Manor were his wife Mary Jane, five daughters with ages ranging from twenty-six to fifteen and one son aged twenty-one, who was a Lieutenant in the 3rd Battalion, Duke of Cornwall's Light Infantry. Also listed are his sister-in-law and a niece.

Attending to the needs of these ten people were, a governess, a butler, a footman, a groom, a cook, two ladies maids, two housemaids, a schoolroom maid, a kitchen maid and a scullery maid. The way of life in this household can only be imagined. What is certain is that Reginald Dykes Marshall, his wife and family served St. John's Church and the town of Keswick, where he lived for over twenty years, in many ways. As Patron of the church he had a part in appointing the four incumbents who followed Canon Battersby. One of them was Reginald Dykes Marshall's cousin, Henry Venn Elliot. He was Vicar for less than three years until 1903 when his health failed. He followed J. N. Hoare whose eighteen years of service covered a great increase in the population of Keswick. The rising congregations meant a lively church and a variety of religious and social activities. H. Gresford Jones was the next appointment but he left after two years to become Vicar of Bradford. He felt that he was called to do more exacting and arduous work than that required at St. John's. Then came the Reverend Morley Headlam who was seven years later to write after the death of Reginald Dykes Marshall in 1913 that the Patron's term of life had covered all the history of the parish of Keswick St. John.

From the magazine of November that year, "No one else can ever take the place he holds in our records. We cannot be too grateful for the way he treasured all his life as a sacred trust, the responsibility with regard to the Church and Parish, which was handed to him by his father so many years ago."

The body was taken back to Leeds to the beautiful Norman Church of Adel very near to the place where his grandfather set up his first mill to spin flax.

The Reverend Morley L. Headlam was instituted as Vicar of St. John's in

December 1906. Coming to Keswick as a bachelor, all his energies were focussed on his new appointment and naturally he expressed his own views and set about making changes. Not surprisingly, some of the views and alterations appear to have disturbed his parishioners.

For many years there had been a surpliced choir of men and boys. When this was established some lady members of the original mixed choir had remained to help with the singing. In the magazine for February 1907, "The choir has needed strengthening in the treble and alto parts. The decision had to be made between increasing the number of lady members, which would be historically a retrograde step, or increasing the number of boys." Apparently the old members relied too much on the ladies! There were some fulsome words of gratitude and the ladies retired, possibly not with great goodwill since later magazines tell of a collection being made for them and a presentation organised. The Vicar only discovered this when it was all over and he had not been asked to be present.

In a short time letters, usually anonymous, and critical of the way Headlam conducted worship were appearing in the public press. There was a correspondent who disagreed with the use of the Prayer Book, and one who objected to the distribution of Palm crosses on the grounds that a palm leaf made into the form of a cross was "undiluted Popery". The vicar replied saying that someone was deceived about what was done and worn at St. John's but he was glad that those who disagreed with the church would say so clearly and come and talk in a friendly way.

A sermon preached on "The Reverence due to the Altar" brought forth further comment and a writer to "The English Churchman" maintained that in recent years incumbents of St. John's had been "a succession of High Churchmen." Headlam was anxious that people should understand. He referred them and also the editors of the The English Churchman and the Mid-Cumberland Herald to the V11th of the Canons of 1640, concerning "the doing of reverence and obeisance both at coming in and going out of Churches, Chancels and Chapel according to the most ancient custom of the primitive Church in purest times". He further reminded them of the conclusion of this Canon "And in the practice or omission of this rite, we desire that the rule of charity prescribed by the Apostle may be observed, which is, that they who use this rite, despise not them who use it not; and that they who use it not, condemn not those who use it."

Varying opinions of ritual practice in churches are continuous but good advice timeless.

Morley Headlam also gave practical directions, expecting the churchyard to be kept tidy, dead flowers removed, the ground levelled, the stones to be simple and the grass kept like a lawn. He also forbade the use of the then fashionable equivalent of today's plastic flowers, which were wax bouquets under glass domes.

As the years went by the Vicar married, settled and became well-loved in his parish.

Of the years preceding the first World War, Winston Churchill wrote "Nearly a hundred years of peace and progress had carried Britain to the leadership of the world. She had striven repeatedly for the maintenance of peace, at any rate for herself, and progress had been continuous in all classes . . . The great mass of the country could get on with their daily tasks and leave politics to those who were interested . . . the dawn of the twentieth century seemed bright and calm for those who lived within the unequalled bounds of the British Empire."

This feeling of confidence and optimism was evident at St. John's as the Reverend Morley Headlam continued his ministry always aided by a curate. The

Mothers' Union was active, sales of work were held to support the library and music flourished. In 1908 Miss Marshall, one of the daughters of Reginald Dykes Marshall, took forty girls to Carlisle for a Music Festival, where they made a very creditable attempt by gaining sixty seven marks out of a maximum of eighty.

A parish tea and entertainment was held in November 1910. The object was both social and a means of raising funds. Various ladies each hosted a table and provided the food. Twenty pounds was the target, to pay the bill for church heating, to provide rooms in the library for Bible study and to erect railings on the south side of the church. The Vicar wrote in his next magazine, "Well: it was a success wasn't it? Did you know before what delightful social people we all are? It was delightful how everyone contributed to the result; the people who gave tea and the people who ate it; the people who told you where to go, and the people who went; the people who stood on the stage and performed, and the people who sat in the hall and clapped. We had a grand time, and even the Churchwardens are pleased." Three hundred and fifty came to tea and after a lyrical account of the occasion he ended by saying that he hoped for five hundred the next year.

Earlier in the same year Morley Headlam had attended a Missionary Conference in Edinburgh and during his time there was present at the Consecration of Dr. Walpole to be the new Bishop of Edinburgh. He could never have envisaged that Hugh, son of the Bishop would be a famous writer, have a home at Brandlehow, on the shore of Derwentwater, worship at St. John's and be buried in the churchyard.

King Edward V11 died and 1911 saw the Coronation of King George V and Queen Mary. Special services were held and it was a day of great celebration. Soon afterwards the suggestion was made that St. John's should be considering a new organ. The original organ was twenty years old, built at a time when experiments in organ building were taking place and had been overused by learners practising. Sometimes, apparently, the sound of the organ was heard all day, as pupils provided part of the organist's income. It was decided that even offering him extra money not to teach was no solution and that a new organ fund should be set up.

Fund raising began and an organ from Harrison and Harrison costing £680 was contemplated. Then it was discovered that if parts of the old one were incorporated only £400 would be needed. By June 1912 sufficient money had been raised and the organ was being built. The plan was to bring as many of the pipes as possible into the chancel arch so that the sound would pass into the main body of the church and not as previously into the north aisle first. The case would be of oak to match the choir stalls. The following year the organ was installed, dedicated and paid for. Optimism continued. After much agitation about the amount of room that should be allowed for comfortable kneeling the seating was renewed and the bell which had rung since 1838 was recast. However war clouds were gathering.

In January 1914 Morley Headlam wrote of the anonymous gift of "a very handsome Cover for our Font" and of the "sweet mellowness of the bell" which had been recast.

By April he was writing under the heading "To Allay Anxiety" that he had been told "there are some who are much distressed because they think that an Altar is to be placed behind the Organ, and that end of the north aisle turned into a side-chapel." He went on to say that there were other people in favour and that he would find it useful. It could be a very convenient and homely little place for daily prayers and for private devotion whereas at that time it was an eyesore with rough deal on the walls and an unsuitable carpet covering dirty boards. He would not, however agree to it until the matter had been considered by the Church Council and the Congregation and a very strong vote of the communicants given in favour.

S. John's Church, Keswick.

PARISH MAGAZINE.

PRICE:—TWOPENCE.

S. JOHN'S PARISH CHURCH.

Rev. CHARLES H. LEWIN, M.A., VICAR, THE PARSONAGE
Rev. E. D. GREGORY, M.A., 43, SOUTHEY STREET.

Mr. J. E. MOORE, F.R.C.O. 21, WORDSWORTH STREET. } ORGANIST & CHOIR MASTER.

Mr. T. T. TOWNLEY, HOLLY BANK.
Mr. A. COWLEY, 12, BLENCATHRA STREET. } CHURCHWARDENS.

Mr. G. TYSON, THE LIBRARY, SEXTON.

J. W. WILLIAMS, PRINTER AND STATIONER, KESWICK.

He concluded "But a side chapel means a side altar, and that is quite a different thing."

War was declared in August 1914. Morley Headlam told the parishioners, "War is awful; awful because of its horrors; but also awful because of its demands. It demands and may never restore to us, our livelihood, our comfort, our friends, our most dearly loved ones; possibly it demands ourselves."

Throughout 1915 the Vicar wrote of the progress of the war but most parish activities went on usual. The side chapel is not mentioned again until April 1916 when plans had been drawn and application was to be made for a faculty. There was still some opposition, not now to the Alter but to the possibility of candles being placed on it at some future date. Eventually, after several meetings ninety-six percent of the congregation agreed that the application should be made but Headlam warned:- The Chancellor may still refuse a faculty. If so, we shall continue as at present until happier times. Small congregations will still seem almost lost in a nave originally estimated to seat between 750 and 800. Old and frail communicants will still have to make their way with anxious and uncertain steps up into and down from the chancel with its dim religious light and celebrants will still have to try and make their cold-enfeebled voices carry to communicants worshipping afar."

Less than a year later the Side Chapel was in use, pews having been removed and the floor levelled. Mr. Axon one of the Churchwardens was evidently a craftsman and was making the Screen. He estimated the cost at £29.19s.5d. and the cost for the Communion rail as £15.

The St. John's Keswick - War Magazine for April 1917 was only one sheet on very poor paper but a paragraph was devoted to the Dedication of the Side Chapel.

"On March 30th, at 12 o'clock, the Bishop of the Diocese dedicated the Side Chapel. He addressed those present and spoke of the great practical and devotional value of a Side Chapel for increasing the sense of fellowship and brotherhood, by bringing individuals scattered over a large Church into a small compact body. He spoke with much appreciation of our Side Chapel, its dignity and its beauty, and bade us remember that GOD'S House and its appointments should always be the most beautiful in the parish".

It was August 1918 before everything to furnish the new chapel had been gifted or paid for. Much of the linen and the Walnut and Silver Cross are in use in church today as is the Silver Chalice, made to a special design, and presented by a Mr. George Bawden whose descendants still worship at St. John's.

In January of that year it was obvious that the war was over and there was rejoicing. Wishing everyone many happy new years Morley Headlam wrote "No other new year has ever begun at St. John's with a Church almost entirely free. Nearly all the pew holders and seat holders have made their pews an offering to our Lord Himself: so that any barrier or distinction, which the possession of private property in the church may have caused is now broken down." Slowly a new social structure was evolving.

The Parish Magazine for January/February 1918, for the first time, featured a photograph of the church on the front. Looking towards the east window, the view was less obscured by trees and bushes but otherwise little different from that seen today, except for the eight graceful pinnacles surrounding the base of the spire. They were similar to those present now on the corners of the east end. (It is believed that during the 1939-45 war one of the tower pinnacles fell down and the others were then taken down for safety reasons). The magazine had just four pages but was printed on better quality paper. A Sunday School Festival on St.

NOVEMBER, 1924.

S. John's Church, Keswick.

PARISH MAGAZINE.

PRICE:—TWOPENCE.

INTERIOR OF S. JOHN'S PARISH CHURCH.

REV. CHARLES H. LEWIN, M.A., VICAR.

MR. C. W. SOWBY, B.A., LAY READER.

MR. J. E. MOORE, 21, WORDSWORTH STREET,   ORGANIST & CHOIR
         MUS. B., F.R.C.O., A.R.C.M., L.R.A.M.   MASTER.

MR. A. COWLEY, 12, BLENCATHRA STREET,   CHURCHWARDENS.
MR. G. BAWDEN, GOVERNOR HOUSE.

MR. G. TYSON, THE LIBRARY, SEXTON.
NURSE STEWART, 18, SOUTHEY STREET, DISTRICT NURSE.

G. W. McKANE, RELIANCE PRINTING WORKS, KESWICK.

John's day was a joyful occasion with a tree given by Mrs. Spedding, who also distributed gifts to the children. Mrs. Marshall, from the Manor, the widow of Henry Cowper Marshall was also present. The infants had their service in the afternoon and were given tea, but due to wartime conditions the older children had to have their teas at home and came for a service later. This was followed by "a very good entertainment, largely produced by themselves."

The vicar, Morley Headlam reported that the Bishop of Carlisle had asked all clergy under forty-five years of age to volunteer as chaplains to the armed forces abroad and those between forty-five and fifty-five to serve at home. He came into the latter category; however, as he had no curate he was not called, but by June of that year he gave his parishioners the news that he would be moving away. The Archbishop of Canterbury had offered him the living of Horsham in Sussex. Reluctantly, he decided to accept. He said that St. John's meant much to him as it was the home to which he brought his bride and the place where his children were born. He wrote "To one who believes in a Divine ordering of things, it seems difficult to believe that an offer coming so unexpectedly and through the official head of the Church was not meant to be accepted."

Morley Headlam and his family left Keswick in the summer of 1918. St. John's magazine for September carries a full account of his institution and induction, by the Bishop of Chichester, at the ancient Parish Church of St. Mary, Horsham. "The bells rang merrily."

The Bishop of Carlisle instituted the Reverend Charles Herbert Lewin as Vicar of St. John's just six days after the Armistice on November 11th. He was to serve for eighteen years and is remembered by some amongst our present church members. His predecessor wrote of him, "Mr. Lewin is a Trinity College, Cambridge man. He was ordained by the Bishop of Durham and worked for 6 years in that Diocese at Bishop Wearmouth and Gateshead. He then spent 9 years in Australia. On his return in 1912 he was for 3 years a member of the York Diocesan Clerical Staff; and for the past 3 years he has been Vicar of S. Paul's, Hull, with a population of about 16,000 people. He is, therefore a man of very wide experience and sympathies; and those who know him speak of him with enthusiasm and affection."

His ministry in Keswick would take place in the years of great change starting at the end of one Great War and almost reaching the beginning of the next.

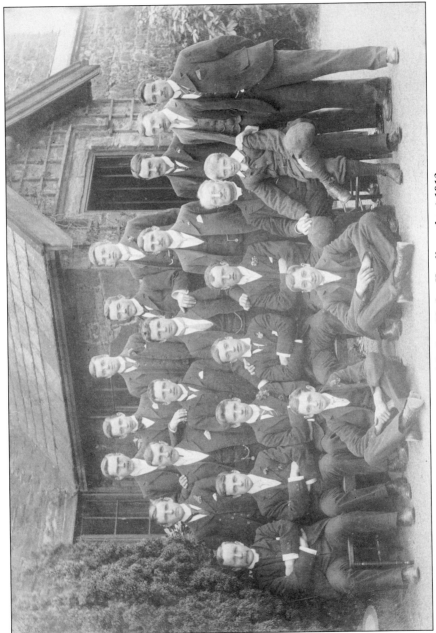

A men's group with vicar Morley Headlam about 1912

Chapter 5

One War to Another, Railways and Heirs

Early in 1919, in only his fourth Parish Magazine Reverend Charles H. Lewin entered the Roll of those from St. John's Parish who had fallen in the War. There were sixty-seven names in this small town and similar rolls would be inscribed on memorials across the country.

The relief of the end of warfare was replaced by anxiety over labour troubles in the country. A railway strike was threatened and Rev. Lewin attempted in his magazine message of October 1919 to clarify the issues for his parishioners. "This is indeed the test of democracy." he wrote, "If the constitutional government of the country is not able to meet the situation then democracy fails. The victory of the strikers, whatever the rights and wrongs of the wage question, would be a disaster for democracy. Is it always wrong to strike? Certainly not, but surely the strikers have to show that this was the only possible course, and that the matter involved was of vital importance, and this is just what according to the papers, they have not done." He went on to say that facts must be faced and a new spirit of brotherhood was needed, based on the teaching of Christ.

In church matters an Enabling Bill passed through Parliament allowing for the election of lay members to the National Assembly of the Church of England. Electoral Rolls should be established in each parish. Those who signed would be able to vote for the Parish Church Council from which representatives could be sent to the Diocesan Conference.

Moving with the times it was decided to initiate a duplex envelope system of giving at St. John's. Rev. Lewin explained that two envelopes joined together would be provided for the weekly offerings, one for the contribution for the work of the church at home and the other for work abroad. The amounts given would be confidential and known only to the Treasurer. This was a change from the days of the previous century when lists of money given and by whom appeared in almost every magazine.

The early 1920s were years when many depended on church life, not only for worship and rites of passage but also for educational and social needs. At St. John's there was a large choir of men and boys which was augmented for special music at Easter and other Festivals. On Good Friday 1921 the augmented choir gave a rendering of Stainer's Crucifixion. Rev. Lewin felt that his congregation was rather timid with singing hymns especially if the tunes were unfamiliar so he instituted Congregational Hymn Practice after evensong on the first Sunday of each month. With choir practices, Band of Hope, Mother's Union, Bible Study and Parochial Teas there was activity and fellowship for all. In summertime many of the parishioners went by train to Seascale on Sunday School Trips. There were donkey rides on the wide golden sands. Some paddled and swam in the sea. They bought postcards and had a picnic before being given a bag of sweets and fruit. There are still some who remember the lovely little seaside town that Seascale then was. Today the wonderful beach is deserted and the Sellafield complex looms menacingly over the town.

The last, and one of the most beautiful of the windows manufactured by Powells of Whitefriars for St. John's was put in place at the west end. The Resurrection window, a memorial to Louise Highton who was a V.A.D. nurse during the war and died aged just twenty, shows the women bringing spices to anoint the body of Jesus and the Angel telling them, "He is not here but risen." Tending the sick and clothing the needy are depicted in the lower portion.

More space was required for burials and a Churchyard Extension Fund was launched to buy and prepare the land below the terrace. In May 1922 the Bishop of Carlisle consecrated the new area.

After the consecration of the new portion of the Churchyard, Rev. Lewin and the

P.C.C. turned their attention to work that was required on the fabric of St. John's. A firm of architects, Messrs. Hicks & Charlwood, reported the necessity to make and keep the Church building dry. "The gutters and spouts are not in good condition and as soon as there is any defect in the lead gutters the water sinks into the Church walls and eventually shows its presence in the discoloured plaster." It was estimated that £1000 would be needed to pay for the work and that a further £1000 would be required to decorate the interior afterwards. A Fund was set up and month by month the total raised was announced in the magazine and some of the work undertaken, but it was 1928 before the renovations were deemed complete.

The members of the Marshall family who were still supporting St. John's were few and the vast fortune that the first John Marshall made had been dissipated. "Marshalls of Leeds Flax Spinners" closed down in 1886 after ten years of losses. The younger members had sought social and political advancement rather than dedication to a changing industrial scene where cotton goods had largely replaced linen. When Henry Cowper Marshall died in 1884 his second son John Marshall III inherited Derwent Island and made his home there. His younger brother Francis or Frank was a housemaster at Harrow. Frank built a house at Hawse End looking across Derwentwater to St. John's and when he retired from teaching was connected with the schools of this parish. He was a Manager from 1907 and Chairman of Managers from 1913-20. He died in 1922 and Rev. Lewin wrote in the Parish Magazine "When most men would have claimed a rest he continued to throw all his energy into everything which would benefit his neighbours and especially all educational work."

The youngest son of Henry Cowper Marshall was William, who went to London and became an architect. In 1888 he had designed the extension to the chancel incorporating the oak choir stalls as a memorial to his father.

After the death in 1913 of Reginald Dykes Marshall, his widow Mary still lived in Castlerigg Manor and continued to be involved in activities at St. John's until she died in 1926. "In everything to do with the church she was deeply interested and always ready to help. Time after time we have heard of her acts of kindness. We are thankful for all that she did for us and for the example of her life, and we desire to express our sympathy with the members of her family which is so closely bound up with St. John's Church" the Vicar wrote in the magazine.

Concern of the family for the church, was then carried on by the daughters of Reginald Dykes and Mary Marshall, in particular, Evelyn Adela. She was deeply involved in the Girl Guide movement at St. John's and throughout the area, becoming County Commissioner for Cumberland.

As representative to the Diocesan Conference she was present in Barrow–in–Furness in 1927, when the subject of a Revised Prayer Book was discussed. Apparently there was much opposition but Miss Marshall was strongly in favour and in the magazine for February asked all who agreed with her to write to their Local member of Parliament. St. John's School also claimed her attention and one lady in our congregation now, can remember Miss Marshall, who died aged eighty in 1954, coming to inspect her needlework.

Eventually the eighteen year long ministry of the Reverend Lewin came to an end. For sixteen of those years his sister, Miss Mildred Lewin had been his companion and helper. She was respected and loved for her work with the Girl Guides, the Mothers' Union, St. John's Nursing Association and various parish organisations. She worked hard to re-organise the Duplex Envelope Scheme and was in charge of the Womens' Bible class. From the Parish Magazine of February 1935, "Keswick will miss her familiar figure and pleasant smile of greeting as she passed up and down the streets." Reverend Lewin must certainly have missed his

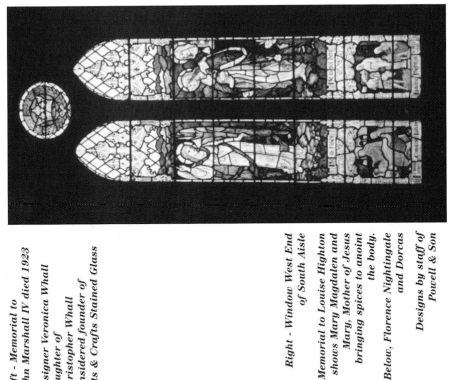

*Left - Memorial to
John Marshall IV died 1923*

*Designer Veronica Whall
daughter of
Christopher Whall
considered founder of
Arts & Crafts Stained Glass*

*Right - Window West End
of South Aisle*

*Memorial to Louise Highton
shows Mary Magdalen and
Mary, Mother of Jesus
bringing spices to anoint
the body.*

*Below, Florence Nightingale
and Dorcas*

*Designs by staff of
Powell & Son*

Castlerigg Manor, Keswick
Home of Reginald Dykes Marshall

sister. His health began to fail and he took a long holiday. He returned only for a short time after which there was a long interregnum.

The Keswick Reminder for June 19th 1936 reports that Helen Marshall performed the Opening Ceremony for St. John's Garden Party. The Parish had been without a Vicar for several months. Speaking about a possible successor to Reverend Lewin, Helen Marshall said that she would like to remind the parishioners of the type of incumbent they had always had at St. John's. Since the early days in her father's time, she remembered it had been said that they wanted a man of wide culture, experience and sympathy for St. John's. She thought they had succeeded admirably in the past. Before long they would have a successor, the kind of man they had always looked for, who would be a leader, spiritual guide, friend and wise counsellor. After other remarks she concluded saying that anything connected with the welfare of St. John's Church, and Keswick would always receive most sympathetic and affectionate consideration from any member of the Marshall family.

Helen Blanche Marshall lived at Threlkeld and died and was buried there in 1946. She played the organ at St. Mary's Church and was one of the most gifted musical personalities in the County of Cumberland. She taught singing as well as Folk and Morris dancing. A skilled needlewoman, she embroidered and gave to St. John's Church, two beautiful altar frontals. These were highly praised by the South Kensington School of Church Embroidery. The white festal frontal was described by them as "a really priceless piece of work, the possession of which any Cathedral might be envious." These are still used regularly, as are the Altar candlesticks, which were her last gift to this church. She presented these in the Centenary year 1938 in memory of her father.

During April 2001 a working party clearing an overgrown corner of St. John's churchyard uncovered a broken memorial cross. When the debris was cleared away it was found to be commemorating the life of Mary Jane (1842-1925) the wife of Reginald Dykes Marshall and two of their daughters. Judging by the condition of the slate stone and the position in the churchyard, it is likely that it was erected after 1954 when Evelyn Adela died. It seems that the damage was caused when a tree was blown down and then undergrowth obscured the cross. The other daughter whose name is on the stone was Rosamund Stewart Lawther (1864-1929).

"A friendly sort of chap, plain spoken like themselves and meaning just what he said and nothing more." With these words the Reverend Herbert Edmund John Mathew introduced himself to his congregation in 1936 when he became the eighth Vicar of St. John's. He was ordained at Chester in 1915 and after a short time as a curate, served as a naval chaplain until 1919. Hyde in Greater Manchester was his first Vicarage, followed by a country parish in Hampshire. When he came to Keswick, Reverend Mathew said that he was glad to be back in a big and busy parish.

A few months later he conducted the funeral of a remarkable lady through whom there was a link with St. John's first incumbent. The body of Eveleen Myers (1856-1937) was brought to St. John's Churchyard to rest beside her husband Frederic William Henry Myers, the eldest son of Henry and Susan Myers. The family graves were just beyond the Parsonage garden, as it was then and the position had a special significance.

Henry Myers had been chosen in 1838 by the Marshall family, to set in motion the life and worship of the newly completed church. His young first wife died after living only a few months in the new home built for them. He must have had sympathy from the brothers and sisters of John Marshall. Together they worked to carry his plans forward after his early death. The youngest sister, Susan,

46

married the widowed Henry Myers and settled in the Parsonage. A son, Frederic William Henry was born in 1843. His immediate surroundings deeply affected this child. In his own words, "It was in the garden of that fair Parsonage that my conscious life began. The memories of those years swim and sparkle in a haze of light and dew. The thought of Paradise is interwoven for me with that garden's glory; with the fresh brightness of a great clump and tangle of blush roses which hung above my head like a fairy forest and made magical with their fragrance the sunny inlets of the lawn - close to the Parsonage is Castlelet, a little hill from which Derwentwater is seen outspread, with Borrowdale in the distance. I can recall the days when that prospect was still one of mysterious glory; when gleaming lake and wooded islands showed a broad radiance bossed with gloom and purple. Borrowdale wore a visionary majesty on which I dared scarcely look too long."

Frederic recounts the first sadness of his childhood when he came upon a dead mole, crushed by a cartwheel, in the road. His mother told him not to grieve because it had no soul, but he wondered. The incident left an impression, which may have contributed to his avowed belief that we live after earthly death.

Frederic William Henry Myers met Eveleen Tennant in London where her mother conducted one of the most successful salons of the day, attracting a wide variety of interesting and important artists, writers and leading political figures. Eveleen was painted by John Everett Millais and her portrait which he considered to be one of his best, was exhibited at the Royal Academy. The marriage took place in 1880 and they moved to a house in Cambridge specially designed for them by Myers' cousin, the architect, William Marshall. They had three children, Leopold (also to become a well-known writer), Silvia and Harold. In 1888, Eveleen took up photography, mainly to record the images of the growing children but became admired as an artistic and innovative photographer whose work was exhibited and used in photographic magazines.

Frederic William Henry Myers died in Rome in 1901. His death is recorded by the Swedish doctor Axel Munthe in his famous book, "The Story of San Michele". Munthe tells of the last words of the dying man. "I am very tired and very happy." Myers had made a pact with his great friend, Professor William James that whichever of them was to die first should send a message to the other as he passed over into the unknown - they both believed in the possibility of such a communication. When the doctor left, William James still sat, grief stricken by the open door, his notebook on his knees. The page was blank.

A memorial tablet was erected in the English Cemetery in Rome but Myers' body was brought home, to be interred in the place beloved since childhood, beside the gate from the Parsonage into St. John's churchyard. Eveleen lived on, a colourful and perhaps eccentric artistic life and is described by a granddaughter as having had "star quality." Thirty-six years after her husband's death her earthly remains were united with his.

The friendly plain spoken Vicar, H. E. Mathew ministered to the Parish throughout the troubled years of the 1939-1945 war. He was interested in the Fitz Park Trust and when he had leisure time liked nothing better than a game of bowls. Playing one day in June 1949, he suddenly became ill and died shortly afterwards. His grieving congregation saw him laid to rest just a few yards from the Myers' tomb.

The inevitable and irreversible changes brought about by the 1939-45 war affected the people of the Parish of Keswick St. John perhaps even more than the 1914-18 war. Many left the area for several years, some never to return. There were others who came into Keswick. Many worshipped here at St. John's, including Basil Tuffield who came to the town with his mother when she decided to leave London. As a young man he worked for the Keswick Urban District Council. He recalls that he appreciated the style of worship and enjoyed the lively social life of St. John's. He found that Herbert Mathew had no server and being used to doing so, offered to take on the regular task. Basil Tuffield remembers his time in Keswick as very formative years and was impressed with the assuring message that the Vicar conveyed to his congregation in times of trouble. After army service he trained for the ministry and was ordained in 1953. Most of his work was in the London area but in 1979 he came back to Cumbria as Vicar of Crosscanonby and Allonby. About five years later he was appointed Rural Dean of Solway and installed as a Canon of Carlisle Cathedral. He retired in 1990.

On 1st February 1950, The Reverend Vorley Michael Spencer Ellis, M.A. was instituted as Vicar of the Parish of Keswick St. John. His ministry was to last for thirty-three years equalling that of Canon Battersby in the previous century. In his first letter to his parishioners Rev. Spencer Ellis spoke warmly of the welcome that he and his wife had received. He continued, "The 'fellowship' of Christ's church must always be a real thing when our religion and worship are a true part of life. In fact, there surely lies the great purpose of a parish church; that it should be the channel through which everything in the parish - trade, business, social life, family life - may be sanctified and offered as an acceptable sacrifice to God; and through that God-ward movement all may see and know that they are indeed members one of another. St. John's is a church with a great tradition, and it is easy to see that it is a church which is much loved."

Those words still ring true but within a few years he was to see changes in the traditional involvement of the Marshall family with St. John's. In 1950 the only surviving active Marshall trustee was Denis of Derwent Island, a grandson of Henry Cowper Marshall. His oldest brother John IV died in 1923, intestate and unmarried. His memorial is the beautiful window in the south aisle, designed by Veronica Whall. The estate passed to the next brother Charles who was involved with the life of the parish and is remembered by Mrs. Margaret Bowden as a kind man, very good with young people. He paid for them to go on many outings. She recalls being in a group taken to Newcastle to see one of the first talkies, Al Jolson in The Singing Fool! When Charles died, Denis inherited all the problems.

Most of the money financing the church endowments was invested in Railway stocks and shares. This was much reduced after the Transport Act of 1947 nationalised the railways. Denis Marshall decided to hand over the endowment to the Diocese. In 1951, he gave Derwent Island and his remaining estates to the National Trust and retired to Sedbergh where he had been a schoolmaster. He must have had very mixed feelings, perhaps satisfaction that the church and the estates would still provide benefits for others as his forbears had always sought to do, but also great sadness and despair. Some of his possessions he destroyed so that they should not pass into unsympathetic hands. There is an apocryphal story that his grand piano was taken out and thrown into the lake. When he died in 1954, St. John's benefited from his legacy of £4000.

Chapter 6

A Family's Trust

From the foundation of St. John's Church by John Marshall in 1838 to the deaths of Denis and Evelyn Adela in 1954, some member of the Marshall family was actively involved in the care of the building, administration, parish organisations, and the welfare of Keswick townspeople. Their memorials are inside the building as windows, brasses and pews. In the churchyard, near to the Vicarage, gravestones mark the resting places of at least twelve of the family. Another great legacy that the Marshalls left for future generations, are the many beautiful mature trees that were planted in the vicinity of the church and around their houses. Active in public life, locally and nationally, wherever the family owned land or homes they founded schools or established village halls, in Patterdale and Loweswater, for example. They served the community as J.Ps and M.Ps yet quite certainly seeking to impose their opinions and no doubt as business people expecting value for money.

John and Jane Marshall had five sons and seven daughters. W. G. Rimmer estimated that by the 1840s there were thirty-eight grandchildren. If so the descendants of John and Jane must now be numbered in hundreds, yet of most of them, nothing is known. Rimmer refers to notebooks letters and correspondence at Derwent Island. Neither the National Trust nor the County Record Office has any knowledge of these archives. It is possible that Denis Marshall disposed of them. Sometimes memories provide clues in oral history but cannot always be checked.

There is, however, some documentary evidence. The County Record Office in Carlisle holds interesting papers deposited there from Hawse End, when the house and grounds became an outdoor pursuits centre. Frank Marshall, a younger son of Henry Cowper Marshall, was a Housemaster at Harrow School and came to live at Hawse End on the western side of Derwentwater when he retired in 1905. His only daughter, Catherine was educated privately, perhaps because of some anxiety about her health, but at home she studied music and languages and helped her mother with the house.

Both Catherine and her mother, were keen suffragette supporters, working with the Women's Liberal Association in Harrow. In 1908, they formed the Keswick Women's Suffrage Association and Catherine became involved with the National Union of Women's Suffrage Societies. In 1911 she was appointed Parliamentary Secretary of the N.U.W.S.S., lobbying to secure a successful women's suffrage Bill in Parliament. The next year she became Honorary Secretary of an election fighting fund aimed at supporting Labour Party candidates in return for the endorsement of women's suffrage as Labour policy. She abandoned the Liberal Party in 1914 and joined the Independent Labour Party, remaining a socialist to the end of her life. A pacifist, she found it impossible to support the war and sought actively for ways to bring it quickly to an end. In 1915 she was one of the organisers of an International Conference of Women at the Hague and subsequently with other pacifist women set up the Women's International League for Peace and Freedom. Although primarily a peace movement they also included as their goals, equal rights between men and women. They were feminist as well as pacifist.

After the war she worked through the W.I.L. for the League of Nations and in 1930's became involved in the plight of Jewish refugees. Some were given asylum at Hawse End. Eventually recognition of the evils of Nazism led her to modify her pacifism. Catherine died in 1961 aged eighty-one.

Here and there through the years, some other members of the family make their mark. With one family there was considerable intermarriage. James Garth and Henry Cowper Marshall both married daughters of Thomas Spring-Rice, first Baron Mounteagle and Chancellor of the Exchequer 1834/9. Widowed, he then married Marianne Marshall. Later, Charles, one of his sons by his first wife, married Elizabeth Margaret, a daughter of William Marshall of Patterdale Hall. Their son, Sir Cecil Arthur Spring-Rice had a home beside Ullswater, near to Hallsteads, John and Jane Marshall's first Lake District property. A distinguished Diplomat and Ambassador to Washington during the 1914-18 war, he acted as a conciliatory influence between Great Britain and the United States and his tact contributed to America joining the Allies. He composed the hymn "I Vow To Thee My Country" and one of his memorials is a bridge over Aira Force.

In 1941 a young man bearing the Marshall name gave his life for his country. W. R. Marshall A'Deane is engraved on the war memorial in Keswick and in Crosthwaite Church. There are recollections by older people in Keswick, that he was from the Patterdale branch of the Marshall family and connected with Richard Marshall J.P. who was living at Lairthwaite in 1929. W. R. Marshall A'Deane commanded the destroyer Greyhound which was sunk by enemy action in the Battle of Crete. He was rescued from the sea by another vessel but dived overboard to try and save the life of a comrade, and was drowned. The Albert Medal was awarded to him posthumously.

In 1788 when John Marshall set up his first flax spinning mill in Leeds or when he came with his young wife, Jane, to stay in Keswick as part of their honeymoon in 1795, he could not have envisaged how their family would prosper and influence social and political life in Leeds, Cumberland, Great Britain and even worldwide. He became an M.P., as did three of his sons. With his sons, he built a modern single storey factory, Temple Mills. It was only the second of its kind in the country, steam heated and the temperature and humidity controlled. The flat roof was covered with turf and sheep grazed on the lush grass. There were baths for the workers (Cold Free, Hot 1d). When the new mill was opened in 1840 there was a great Temperance Tea for the firm's two thousand six hundred workers. Wherever they owned property, the Marshalls built and supported churches, and schools.

John Marshall died in 1845. He would therefore, have seen the Church of St. John the Evangelist in Keswick, built as his second son, John had planned before he died in 1836, and he would have seen his youngest daughter, Susan married to Frederic Myers, the first incumbent. Neither John nor Jane, saw the other church of St. John the Evangelist, built near the Marshall Mills. After Frederic Myers had declined the offer made to him to become Vicar of the Parish Church of Leeds, in order to come to the new church in Keswick, the Reverend Dr. Hook accepted the post. He encouraged the building of new churches in Leeds. During his twenty-two years as Vicar, twenty-one new churches were built. One of these was St. John the Evangelist, which came into being through the generosity of James Garth, and Henry Cowper Marshall, who were then running the firm. They gave £30,000 to build the church and vicarage in Sweet St., to a gothic design of Sir Gilbert Scott. It was completed in 1850 and with another church, St. Barnabas, built by the son of a former associate of John Marshall, served the district, eventually as one united parish, until both were swept away in the great slum clearances carried out in Leeds in the 1930's.

Many of those people displaced were re-housed in the Belle Isle area. With the proceeds from the sale of the sites of the two churches and the transference of the benefices, a new church was built and the Parish of St. John and St. Barnabas, Belle Isle was created. The lectern, pulpit and communion benches from the old St. John's were used in the main church. The altar, reredos and choir stalls furnished the Lady Chapel. Consecration took place in 1939. From a booklet produced in 1988 to celebrate fifty years of the church, the pattern of worship seems to have been High Anglican.

About two years ago, a lady and gentleman walking in St. John's churchyard, spoke to a member of our congregation and mentioned that they were related to the Marshall family. Later, through publicity in our local paper, they contacted me. As far as is known, Louisa Creed, who lives in York with her husband, Lewis, is the only member of the founding family still to value a link with St. John's. Her mother was Elsie Queen Myers (b.1908), married to Kit Nicholson, an architect brother of Ben Nicholson, the artist and sculptor; her grandfather was Leopold Hamilton Myers, a poet and writer (b.1882); her great grandfather was Frederic William Henry Myers (b.1843), whose story with that of his wife, Eveleen has been briefly told. Frederic Myers (d.1851) and Susan Marshall (d.1896) were Louisa's great, great grandparents. So, through Susan, there is a direct blood line back to, her brother, John, our Founder and John and Jane, their parents, who loved this place and bought the land.

Lewis and Louisa Creed

TEMPLE MILL
The magnificent but highly functional
flax spinning mill to your left was
erected by John Marshall, founder of
the Leeds Flax Industry. Joseph Bonomi
modelled it and this office building
(added in 1843) on the Egyptian
temple at Edfu.

Erected 1838-40

Denis Marshall 1876 - 1954
The last of the family to live on the island
Photograph from the Mirehouse Collection
Reproduced by kind permission of John Spedding

MEMBERS OF THE MARSHALL FAMILY

mentioned in

LINEN AND LITURGY

(Dates of Birth and Death where known)

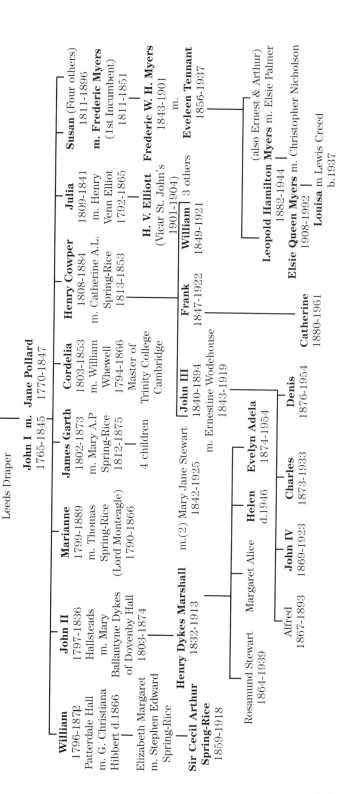

POSTSCRIPT

The last sounds of the opening hymn fade away, priest and choir are in the chancel and the congregation awaits the greeting. "The Lord be with you" and reply "And also with you".

Eucharist, Family Service, Evensong, Songs of Praise may have replaced Holy Communion, Morning Prayer and Evening Prayer. St. Paul may have become "a resounding gong or clanging cymbal" rather than "a sounding brass or a tinkling cymbal" but no translator has changed "Grace, mercy and peace from God the Father and Christ Jesus our Lord".

Fathers of children brought for baptism in 1839 gave occupations such as Bobbin Turner, Ostler, Lead Miner and Nailer. In 1878 there was a Telegraph Clerk, in 1886 a Whetstone Manufacturer, in 1889 along came a Railway Clerk and in 1890 a Railway Porter and a Commercial Traveller. The occupations indicate changing social times but through the years there are Engineers, Farmers, Lawyers, Schoolmasters, Bakers, Joiners and others who might come with their children today.

In the churchyard early monuments are imposing in their individuality; current stones are discreet and uniform. The burial place of the Myers family is a solid table tomb. Henry Cowper Marshall's memorial is a massive sandstone cross in the Celtic style but with none of the delicacy usually associated with such designs. His son lies beneath a stone similar to those given to Crusaders, yet his grandson, Denis, the last Marshall to inhabit the island home, has a very simple gravestone. There has been change in the way people, or those remembering them felt about their place in society and what was considered appropriate in each generation.

Those who once carried along the life of the church are remembered all around it, in ever increasing numbers. There are the Battersbys, the Hightons, the Thorntons, the Hodgsons, the Knights, who with many other whole families worked alongside the Marshalls. There are those who achieved fame yet still counted it a privilege to give time and energy to St. John's. James Clifton Ward, Geologist and Curate; John Postlethwaite, Mining Engineer and collector of fossils; Hugh Walpole, Novelist son of a Bishop. There are war graves of young servicemen and a Roll of Honour in the War Memorial on the north aisle. One by one veterans and members of the British Legion are being laid to rest, including recently, Commander William Spooner Donald, a naval hero, who read the lessons with a strong clear voice until a few years before he died at the age of ninety-one.

As lives end other lives begin and the tiny tots who play in the south-west corner, the young girls in the choir and the boy servers are the ones who will carry on the trust of the founders.

The service is over, the reassuring words of a Post Communion prayer heard and a blessing received. Choir and Clergy process back down the nave with a resounding recessional hymn.

Go in peace to love and serve the Lord.

In the name of Christ Amen.

May the souls of the faithful departed through the mercy of God, rest in peace.

And rise in glory.

SOURCE MATERIAL

Book of the Records of the Trustees of Keswick St. John. County Record Office, Carlisle.

Parish Registers, Keswick St. John.

St. John's Keswick Parish Magazines, 1884-1951. Surviving copies in bound volumes with Crosthwaite Parish Magazines, 1884-1904, 2 vols. St. John's Keswick Magazines, 1885-1935, 3 vols. Other existing Parish Magazines to 1951.

SELECT BIBLIOGRAPHY

Allibone, J.	Anthony Salvin, Pioneer of Gothic Revival Architecture. Lutterworth 1987
Betjeman, J.	Guide to English Parish Churches. Revised J. Kerr 1950
Bott, G.	Keswick, The Story of a Lake District Town Cumbria Supplies and Chaplins 1994
Fraser, D. (ed)	A History of Modern Leeds. M.U.P. 1980
Harford Battersby Brothers	Memoir of T. D. Battersby. Seeley & Co. 1890
Lion Handbook	History of Christianity 1977
Lockhart, J. G.	The Life of Sir Walter Scott, Bart. Black 1893 (p564)
Munthe, A.	The Story of San Michele. Murray 1929
Myers, F.	Catholic Thoughts on the Bible and Theology Pub. privately. 1841-8. Collection of Sermons preached at St. John's, 1838-48, Pub. privately
Myers, F. W. H.	Fragments of Prose and Poetry. Ed. E. Myers Longmans Green 1904
Nicholson and Burn	History and Antiquities of West Cumbria. Vol. II 1777
Rimmer, W. G.	Marshalls of Leeds Flax Spinners 1788-1886 C.U.P. 1960
Sloan, W. B.	These Sixty Years. Pickering & Inglis 1934
Trevelyan, G. M.	Illustrated English Social History. Vol. IV Longmans, Green 1949-52
Wordsworth	The Letters of William and Dorothy Wordsworth ed. By E. de Selincourt. 3 vols. 1935-39

LEAFLETS

National Trust	Derwent Island.
Pickett, M.	The Parish Church of St. John and St. Barnabas, Belle Isle 1938-1988 Published by the Vicar and Churchwardens 1988
Smith, D. I. Carvers	James and George Brooker: West Cumberland Ship of the Mid-19th Century. Trans. C.W.A.A.S. Vol. C. 2000
Spencer-Ellis, V. M.	The Parish Church of St. John, Keswick
Watson, R.	St. John's Parish Church: A Guided Tour
ALSO:	Census Records Files of the **"KESWICK REMINDER"** 1935-1949 Leeds Mercury Supplement 1892 Notes and Quotes, Leeds Mercury 1924 **Directories of Cumberland** Mannix and Whellan 1847, Bulmers 1901, Kellys 1910

A GUIDED TOUR
OF
THE PARISH CHURCH
OF
KESWICK ST. JOHN

To begin your tour stand in the central aisle below the west gallery, facing the altar.

The site for this church was chosen by the founder, John Marshall, Lord of the Manor of Castlerigg and son of a Leeds linen manufacturer. He was a friend of William Wordsworth who influenced his choice of the position, ensuring that the graceful spire might be seen from miles around. It would become a constant witness to Almighty God in an area of great natural beauty.

The architect was Anthony Salvin (1799-1881). The material he selected for the outer walls was a soft pink sandstone from quarries in the Eden valley but the main structure was of local stone. In 1836 when the building was in its early stages, John Marshall died leaving a wife, Mary and a young son Reginald Dykes Marshall. Mary decided that the plans for the church should be carried forward as a fitting memorial to her husband and she met the whole cost of the building herself, £4000. Hugh Percy, the Bishop of Carlisle, consecrated the newly built church and churchyard on St. John's Day, **December 27th 1838.** Later the remains of John Marshall were interred below the centre aisle of the nave.

The Building, in the Old English style, originally comprised the west tower and spire and what is now the central nave and the vestry. The east end of the church was just beyond the first window on the south side of the present chancel across to where the organ is now situated on the north side. The east window and the side windows were plain glass with a coloured border and the furnishings consisted of a stone pulpit and font with a communion table and a reading desk.

In 1862 The building was enlarged and a north aisle was added by introducing columns and arches to support the roof and moving the walls and windows outwards. Twenty years later the south aisle was constructed to match and, in 1889 the chancel was created by moving the east wall outwards, raising the floor above the level of the nave, and moving the sanctuary and altar onto a higher level.

Move to your right to the south aisle to look at the stained glass windows and memorials.

The South Aisle contains an interesting selection of stained glass. At either end of the aisle there are windows associated with the Highton family. The window at the east end is a memorial to the first headmaster of Brigham School, Thomas Highton. The resurrection window at the west end is in memory of his grandaughter, a V.A.D. nurse in the 1914-1918 Great War.

Face the south wall. From the west end the other stained glass windows are:-

1. The modern window commemorates the seven years ministry of Canon Richard Watson who died suddenly while on a pilgrimage to Iona in 1990. It was given by his family, friends and parishioners of Keswick. Christine Boyce of Brampton, Cumbria was the designer.

2. The single light of Jesus inviting children to come to him is in memory of Joseph Thornton (1849-1889), a churchwarden and servant of St. John's. The designer was Henry Holiday and the work executed by James Powell and Son.

3. The window with children dressed in 1920's style clothes, surrounding Jesus, shows one child holding a ball and another pulling a toy wagon. The designer was Veronica Whall (1887-1967) who used rich and glowing colours and with excellent craftsmanship uses the lead as an integral part of the picture. It is a memorial to John Marshall (died 1923) a grandson of Henry Cowper Marshall. John Marshall of Derwent Island and his younger brothers helped to establish the National Trust.

4. The last window, showing St. John and St. Paul commemorates the life of Reginald Dykes Marshall, son of the founder. He died in 1913 after seventy-five years as patron of this church. The maker was again James Powell and Son, the stock figures were drawn by a member of their studio called Read.

In the centre of this aisle is the imposing marble memorial to Thomas Dundas Harford Battersby, second vicar of this parish, who in 1875 held three days of Meetings for the Promotion of Christian Holiness, using tents in the Vicarage grounds. The annual Keswick Convention was established from this humble beginning and continues to this day from a permanent Convention Centre in Skiddaw Street, under the title **"All One in Christ Jesus"**.

To the right of the Battersby memorial is a list of the Vicars of this parish.

In **1938,** when the church centenary was celebrated, pews of Austrian oak were fixed throughout and this aisle was made a memorial aisle with the names of members of many local families, who have worshipped here, carved on the ends of the pews.

Continue round to the centre of the church past the stone font and eagle lectern to look at the chancel and sanctuary.

The Chancel and Sanctuary contain many interesting features. The first organ was installed and the finely carved oak choir stalls erected in memory of Henry Cowper Marshall of Derwent Island, a brother of the founder. In 1912, the organ was rebuilt by Arthur Harrison of Durham and is considered to be one of the finest small church organs in the North of England. It was completely restored in 1990.

The Old English style riddell posts crowned by candle bearing angels were added to the altar about 1920.

The original stone font has been moved from its traditional position at the north west end of the church to the edge of the chancel. The font cover was made at the Keswick School of Industrial Arts.

The eagle lectern was carved by a parishioner, George Brooker and presented to the Rev. J. N. Hoare in 1887. Brooker was from a West Cumbrian family of wood carvers. One of his skills was making figureheads for ships. Another carver, John Milburn made the base.

Stand between the choir stalls to view the stained glass windows.

The wonderful east window is seen at its best early on a sunny morning. Reginald Dykes Marshall commissioned the artist Henry Holiday to design the window as a memorial to his father, John Marshall, whom he would scarcely be able to remember. Holiday (1839-1927) was the principal designer for the London firm of Powell and Sons. The window was fixed by them in 1879, the total cost being about £500. At the time the firm was experimenting with fluxes to fix the colour to the glass. It was not entirely successful and some of the pigment has not worn very well. When the chancel was being extended in 1889, the stained glass was taken out by Powells. The east wall was demolished, rebuilt and the glass put back again.

The lower figures represent Old Testament stories. From left to right, Naaman, Ruth, Isaac, Jonah, Isaiah and David. Above them are New Testament scenes, Christ and Nicodemus, Christ and the Woman of Samaria, The Crucifixion, The Resurrection, Christ Healing the Blind and Christ Charging Peter to "Feed My Lambs".

The other chancel windows were supplied in 1889 by Powell and Sons, using Holiday's designs. Either side of the sanctuary, the windows showing the four evangelists, Matthew, Mark, Luke and John were given by the Marshall family. They are memorials to members of the family who carried on the intentions of the founder. Susan, youngest sister of the founder and Widow of the Rev. Frederic Myers, the first Vicar of this church, arranged for the window opposite the organ to be installed in memory of her husband. Possibly the best window in design and execution it shows three of Jesus' parables - The Lost Piece of Silver, The Good Shepherd and The Sower.

Retrace your steps and as you re-enter the nave, note in front of you the initials J.M. carved into the slate floor where the founder is buried.

Look upwards towards the west end of the nave to view the seven paintings of Celtic Saints. These delightful representations were painted by Sister Irene of the Community of the Holy Name. She was Parish Sister at St. John's for ten years until 1998. Some sisters of the Community of the Holy Name live in the old parsonage, now known as Holy Name House.

Turn right past the original stone pulpit into the north aisle.

A Side Chapel was created in 1917. In November 2000 this was altered by using a screen which was formerly between the pulpit and the first pillar separating the nave and north aisle. The oak screen was erected there in 1894, by John Milburn, a craftsman and Churchwarden 1891-1893, in memory of his son Jonathan who died aged twenty-one in 1892. The wood was accurately matched to provide a rear wall for the present chapel and the altar and aumbry brought forward. Behind the wall there is now a spacious choir vestry. The **Lady Chapel** is used for weekday services and is a quiet place for private prayer.

In the centre of the **North Aisle** wall is the carved oak memorial to those from this parish who died in two world wars. A book containing their names is in an illuminated cabinet where the pages are turned regularly.

Hanging above the north aisle is a banner depicting the young Saint Herbert who lived on an island in Derwentwater during the seventh century. It was created by an internationally renowned sculptress, Josefina de Vasconcellas who was born in Brazil and has lived in Cumbria most of her life.

Outside, below the west tower you can enjoy one of the finest views around Keswick. At the south end of the terrace is the grave of novelist, Sir Hugh Walpole who attended this church when he was in residence at Brackenburn on the west side of Derwentwater.

Thank you for coming. We pray you leave with a blessing.

INDEX

INDEX (continued)